SEARCHING FOR CLOVES AND LILIES

SEARCHING FOR CLOVES AND LILIES

The Wine Edition

REGINE T ROUSSEAU

ABOUT SEARCHING FOR CLOVES AND LILIES: THE WINE EDITION

The first edition of *Searching for Cloves and Lilies* was published in 2010. These poems emerged when I started asking friends and strangers, "What's your favorite body part?" Most people answered my question and opened up to me. Others just smiled and laughed at my question; they shook their heads and left it to my imagination. I took in their answers and their silences and created these poems. As the poems developed their own lives and their own body parts, they moved through and beyond the physical realm.

After publishing *Searching for Cloves and Lilies*, I returned to the book at least once a year. With every reread, I am struck by how alive these poems are, how they continue to evolve, and how they evoke the same emotions year after year. I wondered if my subjects would have the same answers years later. Would new poems come from their answers? Every year, I confirmed that I didn't want new answers, but I knew a second part was coming.

When I met the World Wine Guys on a wine trip to Ribeiro, a region in Galicia, Spain, I quickly fell in love with them. We talked about our mutual passion for wine and experience in the wine business, and the conversation turned toward my book.

"You should pair the poems with wines."

There it was! The suggestion struck me like a lightning bolt. Wine—like my poems—develop their own lives and tell their own stories. Wine moves through and beyond the physical to evoke an emotional response. This time I returned to the poems, and I focused on their personalities. I found their quietness, boldness, simplicity, and complexity and connected them with wines that matched their nature.

In this collection, I've merged my two loves, and I offer these pairings to you.

...What will your search bring you in these pages?

ACKNOWLEDGMENTS

To God be the Glory.

To the World Wine Guys, for their mentorship and willingness to give.

Contributing Sommeliers: Wanda Cole, Advanced Sommelier and Brian Duncan, Down To Earth Wine Concepts, LLC for providing insight into the pairings and hours of education.

Special thanks to The Cloves and Lilies Society (you know who you are) for your vulnerability, tears, time, encouragement and honesty.

Lyrics from the songs of Boukman Eksperyans, the Haitian musical group, appear in the poems "Crossroads" and "After the Quake." Their music has been a source of inspiration and has kept me connected to my roots. Incorporating the works of this legendary group is a way of honoring my Haitian ancestry and creating a legacy.

CONTENTS

Part 3 **Blue Nudes**

MUSES

Thank you, Muses.

Did you know you were inspiring poetry when you were still—when you laughed, flipped your hair, or played?

I could have written novels about your love, your power, your lashes, or the palm of your hand.

I know you and thank you all for the gift of that knowing.

PART 1
AGITATION OF THE WATERS

Who will love my darkness; the parts that I keep hidden, the parts that are not loveable?

I begin this chapter with Psalm 139 because these poems expose the hidden and ask, "Who will love my darkness?" I paired it with the mysterious Château Musar Red. The wine starts off secretive. So tight and closed that its essences are difficult to identify. You have to be patient, get past its darkness, wait for it. When the wine decides; at ten, twenty, thirty, perhaps sixty minutes after it relaxes and breathes, the wine's secrets are revealed. Vulnerability expressed as the aroma of violets; brokenness imaged in the aftertaste of dried herbs, longing in the layers of dark-red fruit and hope in a bright cherry finish.

PSALM 139

You have searched me,
And you know me.
You know when I sit and when I rise;
You perceive my thoughts from afar.
Before a word is on my tongue,
You know it completely, O Lord.
You hem me in behind and before—
You have laid your hand upon me.
Where can I go from your spirit?
Where can I flee from your presence?
I say, "Surely the darkness will hide me,
And the night becomes light around me."
Even the darkness will not be dark to you;
The night will shine like the day,
For darkness is light to you.

CROSSROADS

"Crossroads" was inspired by a work of art by Artist Jeff Maldonado. I was asked to create a poem that responded to Maldonado's image of a Native American man with a stern face and sad spellbinding eyes. Something about his image reminded me of my partner at that time. His eyes were also melancholy. I did not yet know the source of his sadness and how it would shatter our relationship. I wrote this poem to give voice to the unknown that lingered beneath our picture-perfect life. I paired "Crossroads" with the Yalumba Eden Valley Viognier. The pairing came easily because beneath the serenity of this wine there exists an agitation that draws you in. Notes of gravel follow flavors of white flowers. Ginger root trails peach and pineapple is carried by thyme.

Time crumbles beneath our bed.
Centuries tremor through the
Earth in screams.
Listen for the seconds

                Time crumbles beneath our bed.
                Centuries tremor through the
                Earth in screams.
                Listen for the seconds

"Samba sa fem mal O.
mwen rèl
Samba ma rèl.
Samba sa fè mal."

                "god, this hurts."
                I am crying out, "god,
                god, this hurts."

Stormy skies rip summer from
Love's memory.
Bass echoes misery.
"Samba sa fè mal O."

Stormy skies rip summer from
Love's memory.
Bass echoes misery.
"god, this hurts."

"Na woule Samba, Na woule.
Samba sa fè mal O.
Gade sa neg yo fè m 'san mwen ap koule.
Yo ban m 'yon chay pou pote. Chay la lou Chay-la lou o anwe
M'pasa pote. Anwe."

"I will keep moving forward,
Moving. god, this hurts.
Look what they have done to me. My blood is spilling.
They've given me a burden to carry. It's too heavy. The bur-
den is too heavy. I can't carry it."

O non du Pere, du Fils, et du Sante Esprit.
     In the name of the Father, the Son, and the Holy Spirit
A lost soldier surrenders.
We fear the laughter of fallen angels.
"Nous pe woule Samba.
Nous pe woule Samba."

A lost soldier surrenders.
We fear the laughter of fallen angels.
"We are moving forward, god.
We are moving forward, god."

Mute trees bend to
Comfort empty veins.
Howling for mercy.
You are liquid.
I carved poinsettias on his arms
As a Soprano surrenders to ecstasy.
This is music to God's ears.

Mute trees bend to
Comfort empty veins.
Howling for mercy.
You are liquid.
I carved poinsettias on his arms
As a Soprano surrenders to ecstasy.
This is music to God's ears.

Au nom du père, du fils et de saint l'esprit
In the name of the Father, the Son, and the Holy Spiri

Our fingers brushed between lives. Kite m montre ou parade.
Our fingers brushed between lives. Let me show you
paradise.
Psst, psst.
My soul curls from his lips.
I am released to seduce another.

Psst, psst.
My soul curls from his lips.
I am released to seduce another.

Soul mates dance at the crossroads of heaven
Soul mates dance at the crossroads of heaven

ABOUT HIM AND ME

There was a moment when we were so confident in our love, that we were deaf to words of caution. No one's doubt, not even our own could shake us. Here is that moment coupled with the Inman Family Endless Crush®. A wine fresh and full of life with tickling acidity! This wine makes me schoolgirl happy. Flirtatious with ripe watermelon and strawberry notes, this wine feels free and careless, like our beginning.

One hand chases the other,
So our stream cannot be slowed.
Between the ticking of the hands and
The agitation of the waters,
Words timber
In this, our deaf forest.
Hurry fast, oh Lord…this
Avalanche cometh.
Naked—our knees locked
Front to back, one on top of the other,
We crawl the steps of St. Peter.

SHARON (HAIR STYLIST) AND DAVE (BARBER)

Sharon (Hair Stylist) and Dave (Barber), are one of my favorite couples. She never revealed her favorite body part. I wrote this piece to celebrate how this couple support and nurture each other's passions. They are grounded and certain of who they are as individuals and as a family. Their wine match, Kendall Jackson Vintner's Reserve Chardonnay. A fruit-forward wine with a firm structure that whips flavors of banana, butter, and oak into a golden libation that melts the hearts of classic California Chardonnay lovers.

She lay all day.
     Our hair—
     Butter whip.
     Sorrows snip and weave our
     Shortcomings into Goldilocks's fantasies.
She lies at night, strand by strand.
     Irons heat
     Over him.
     Hot,
     They whip
     Like butter melts.

DOT

"Dot" is a poem about the end of a relationship, when his darkness came to light. My emotional state was like the Allegrini Amarone. It has a dark, intense, and heavy beginning that softens, given time. Amarone is made from grapes that are traditionally dried for more than one hundred days. Waiting for the seasons of this relationship to change was challenging...but like the one-hundred-day drying process of Amarone, actualization and maturity require time and patience.

My italic lover breathes cool phrases up my skirt,
and summer turns to fall. There is no chance of rain,
only suspicious breezes that carry memories of heat waves.
My leaves are electric, stubborn, and refuse to change color.
I wish I could shake your confession loose from trees
But keep the lessons and the lovers that helped me pass the
seasons you were gone.
I squeeze in between parentheses in search of reason but find
that there is a period at the beginning of we.
Autumn, a nagging mother who will not let us forget,
cries and grunts an inebriated winter. Days are long and laced with
curses of summer
heat that dried the hyphen between you and me.

You offer stories of floods that baptized you anew...
ellipses, I am spring, you propose. But I have lost faith in daisies; they
are
fragile and withered from rage.

CORAZON

Have you ever witnessed a liar's unraveling? The reveal begins soft, sweet and rational, "I was going to tell you". Then there is an explosion and the truth leaks. Paired with Domaine Zind-Humbrech Gewurztraminer Turckheim, wine that draws you in with a seductive aroma of rose petals and spices. The palate is equally alluring with notes of sweet tangelo and orange peel. The bitterness of truth comes at the wine's finish with a callous, unexpected sharpness of grapefruit peel.

The chambers of his heart are filled with sleeping men.
"I do."
They hum evening wishes and howl from his mouth like secrets
trapped beneath the tongue.
"I do."
Two years later,
A dam breaks, and silence shines, screaming waves of truth.
"I was going to tell you."
God cowers at the corner of his heart.
Love walks on broken glass, crushing vows.
"This is too much pain."
And then six months later,
An offer of tears in cupped hands for mercy,
The pond overflowing, and I drink from addiction.
There is no restoration without penance.
Still today,
I linger at the corner of his eye, aching from memories.

VODKA AND TONIC

On the first sip, the Conundrum White seems laid back and simple. You can get so hooked on its sweetness that you miss the commotion this blend of Chardonnay, Sauvignon Blanc, Semillon, Muscat Canelli and Viognier will cause. Like the push and pull in the relationships described in "Vodka and Tonic," the flavors in this wine will seduce and abandon.

Clinks of crescent-shaped ice filling a glass begin the ceremony. An end-of-the-day bell for you…fingernails on a blackboard to me. I am your altar boy. I handle each short cocktail glass like a chalice. I bring forth vodka, tonic, lime (always in that order) with the grace of a gaping worshipper.

Our service is nondenominational; we make use of all religions. A hymn, we make an offering; an hour later, you are up by two drinks, and the baptism begins. I am praise dancing and gospel singing as you bear witness to the power of the Holy Ghost. *"I know it was the blood—I know it was the blood for me, for me. One day when I was lost…"*

Preaching wasn't necessary back then; we were new saints and moved on with the confession.

This is our favorite part. Babe, I am not worthy to receive you…I confess to you and to God…heal me…We believe in…God grant me the serenity…I have sinned through my own faults…We absolved each other of our sins, promised to love like Christ and toasted to our future.

We must have spoken in tongues.

I get anxious around five o'clock and hide in the garage as long as I can. The service now begins without me. You find more devout worshipers—neighbors, who listened through cracked walls for the school bell. Their eyes stay close to me; they are experienced and see my plans to leave the cult. Come with me.

JAMAICAN BASS PLAYER

This poem makes me laugh. It is an ode to the upright bass, the sexiest instrument to watch a man play. I paired it with the Antinori Chianti Classico Riserva. I recently wrote a review of the wine and described it thus: "So good I want to stick my face in the glass and French-kiss it." This wine is warm and velvety on the tongue, with fresh herbs on the nose and Chinese five-spice powder on the palate. Yes. Please. And thank you!

Play me
Like that upright bass.
Cradle me.
Rock me.
Sustain me
Against your chest.
Dip me.
Tip me.
Do re me
While you pluck my cords
Into a rat-a-tat-tat.
Tonight, I'll moan in scat.

HE TURNED THE CORNER

This poem is inspired by an ex-lover who loved both another woman and me. My favorite line in this piece is, "I searched the air for your scent of cloves and lilies." Now, which wine? I knew the smell of cloves would come from barrel aging—but lilies? So I phoned a friend for help… how could I forget my favorite Viognier? My search led me to the E. Guigal Condrieu an oak-aged viognier. The clove notes and the signature flowers work in perfect harmony. I was his clove and she his lily. Maybe the choice of spice or flower is impossible. Who can live without both?

You missed my transformation; I turned the corner about a block after you ran into us—Elizabeth and me. We were a pretty picture. Admit it. You pretended not to see, but I caught my reflection in your sadness.

My memory was a mirror, vain and shattered, and needed her likeness. Besides, I didn't think you and I would photograph as well.

You missed my transformation; I looked back about a minute after you drove off, through the red. I searched the air for your scent of cloves and lilies and found it on my fingers. Our afternoons linger in my skin and threaten to expose my weakness. I love you, but want her to be you, looking like her, but I love you. Babe, I love you.

We are frozen in the scratch of this broken record.

Your leaving transformed me.

CREEPIN'

The line "make my summer twelve months long" was the inspiration for choosing Coto de Gomariz, "The Flower and The Bee" Treixadura. This wine is sunshine in a glass— it has a creamy texture, flavors of fresh citrus, pink lady apple, tropical fruits and honey. Simply magical, like this foolish summer romance.

Carolyn, your husband! Your...husband. Your husband
Makes my summer twelve months long, midnight
Early, and my lunch breaks three hours short.
Shit.
Who needs a job?
When he pays attention, we
Eat each other and sleep in
Your bed. He makes the gospels music,
Dinner—occasionally—and Sundays yours.
So I go to church.

THE WORLD OF LOST LOVERS

This is a reflective piece that tries to understand why men vanish (or ghost) from relationships. The perfect balance to this poem is Brown Estate Vineyards Chaos Theory—a powerful blend of Zinfandel, Cabernet Sauvignon, and Petite Sirah. It's a love-at-first-sip wine that will take your palate on a roller-coaster ride of blackberries, bacon fat, eucalyptus, and black pepper. Like the behavior of men, this wine is unpredictable.

I imagine, in the moments after the heat of last night, when he lies, "I've got an early-morning meeting," the earth opens and swallows our lovers. How else do you explain their disappearance?

They arrive at our places late, apologetic, and fragmented. We see them fading in the pauses between "You were supposed to be here an hour ago" and "I need you to understand my feelings." "Sister, save yourself." Thank you, Iyanla, Dr. Phil, Gary Z, and of course, Ms. Oprah.

We are hopeful that our fingers will glide along their chests and connect dots into clear pictures of we and us. And when fingers fail, we use tongues and tricks taught by too-long-ago Charles. Whatever happened to him? We search time for his mark on our chastity belt. Was he number fifteen or sixteen? Our good girlfriends will know.

Moans, oh Gods, and desire for liquid. They exhale. Our desperation escapes and echoes a whispered prayer—"Please stay the night."

The sound of our floors creaking below their weight alarm us that night is surrendering to dawn. Sunlight, our prayers fall on deaf ears. "I've got an early-morning meeting. I'll call you."

I imagine that "I'll call you" is the "open-says-me" that cracks the earth to make room for our lovers to escape. I imagine that in our absence, these men have created a world, comfortable and mute, where they can hide from…us? I see big leather couches, phones off the hook, and endless refrigerators. Who gets the beer?

I wonder if we made a mistake, in between strokes and cooking dinners and listening to their stories, as we disclosed our expectations. Were they listening between innings? I imagine they heard us fearfully pleading "Hold me, love me, and rock the baby" but preferred to be swallowed.

"WHAT IF I CAN'T" is written over the doorway to the world of lost lovers. We women don't know this. So we grieve over stained sheets, wondering, "What did I do? How many more?" And we write poems.

Who speaks for our lovers? I imagine that they sit mute on their couches, wishing for last nights, fingers, and tongues, but are too afraid to call. "What if I can't" sirens loud in their ears.

I see this and have learned to shift shape. Sometimes I am the earth, wide open, and make room for him to fall. Sometimes I am the couch and let him sit quietly. Sometimes I am sound and scream, "You can."

And he does.

PART 2
AND YOU AND YOU AND YOU

MUMMY

My mother is both skeptical and hopeful about love. Her counsel is both sweet and biting. I paired her poem with the Emilio Lustau Los Arcos Amontillado Sherry. This wine captures her conflict: there's the sweetness of raisins juxtaposed with the saltiness of nuts. The wine is mature yet bright, soft, yet dry. This is my Mummy.

My mother reads dreams. She predicts that I will never find love. I call her every morning to read mine. Some mornings I make them up. I want her to be wrong. Some mornings she amuses me, listens, but never lies. "It means you think your mother is an old fool." This morning, I called early, "Mummy, I dreamed..." What do you think it means? This one needed no interpretation; I wanted to be wrong. I cursed my abbreviated love line. "Men is not for us; turn your life to God," she says, unmoved. I know her prophecy hurts her more than me. She, too, prayed that you would break this cycle.

SHE CRIES ON THE GREEN LINE

This poem was inspired by a Facebook post where my friend described the sadness of passengers on the Chicago El train as so palpable that it brought her to uncontrollable tears. I accompanied this poem with the Silice red wine from Ribeira Sacra D.O. At first sip, the wine surprises with the taste of puckering sour cherry balls, then gathers strawberry and finishes with calming notes of pomegranate. Drinking this wine takes you through the emotional release of a good cry.

On the Green Line train,
Kelly cries for the shoulders inches from a friendly brush,
Stiffening to maintain a disconnection.
She cries for the hands grasping silver poles
For balance while aching to slide down to a dirty dance.
She cries for the motionless faces a breath's distance from comfort.

She cries from the pain of the heaviness of our shoulders,
Sees the solitary hand's struggle, and
Hears the sigh of our breath,
Aching to tickle lashes.

She cries...
On this morning's news, I heard that "a study by Israel's Weizmann Institute of Science says women's tears send a chemical signal that triggers sexual disinterest in men."
My life's study tells me that the tears of women who love enough to listen for the grunts of our shoulders, hear the cries of our hands, and sighs of our breath are ointment for our souls.

BRENDA'S EYES

Brenda's favorite body part is her eyes. They are entrancing as they change color from gray to turquoise. I am also captivated by the hue of Movia Lunar 8 Ribolla (orange wine): deep amber-orange, bright gold and sunrays. The blend of shades is as captivating as the wine's woody, spicy, herbal and clementine flavors.

> A peacock blooms
> In the turquoise of closed lids—
> Lashes like feathers
> Flirt between blinks.
> Here is the beginning
> And end of rainbows.

PASTOR LEON PERRY III

As a friend and pastor, his words have always provided guidance and comfort. Pastor Perry has taught me to break from fear. Leon Perry has taught me to walk towards happiness. His lessons are enhanced by the cozy feel of the Casa Ferreirinha "Papa Figos" Tinto, Douro. This wine is spiritually gratifying with silky tannins and soothing red fruit.

I tried to break camp
Around midnight,
Afraid of the cost
Of crossing the Jordan.
I am no Joshua.
I thought you were sleeping
And would not hear me
Gathering psalms and proverbs
For my journey.
How long did you trail me
Before I heard your command to
Fall in.
Grace leaped forward,
And I found myself marching
At the center of a river.

THAT BROTHER THEY CALL "D"

"That Brother They Call 'D'" takes a humorous view on being "ghosted." I paired this poem with the Maison Noir O.P.P Pinot "Noir." I love how this winery produces excellent wines but doesn't take itself too seriously. When your lover ghosts, you can either laugh or cry. Sometimes you have to laugh...O.P.P (Other People's Pinot Noir) is a bright, playful delight with pretty red cherry fruit and an earthy and even palate.

I, Divine Diva, denounced desire.
Dented from Dan, Doug, and other Dogs,
Till "D" day at dusk,
Detoured that brother they called "D."
We dialogued deeply,
Discussing dogma, doo-wop,
And disappointing daddies.

You disclosed dreams,
And I
Dared drown.

As Diana and Duke duet(ted),
We danced dirty,
Dictating delicious don'ts.
"Damn, dear, is that dick detachable?"
Doubled over with laughter,
You dug deep into my darkness,
Discovered dungeons,
As we drifted into daylight.
You disclosed dreams,

and I
designed diamond.
Disremembering,
I, Diva, Divine, went down—
dangled, doted,
and invited you to dine. D'oh!
Did I seem desperate?
You dashed on, Delta—
did not dial,
disconnected, disappeared.
And I dismissed.

PAPPY

I selected the Rodolfo Art of Andes Tannat because, like my Pappy, the wine has an earthy, rustic quality. Like my father, the finish just won't give up.

My father, my father,
My father at age five, so young,
You collapsed.
Your childhood, amputated,
Crept belly down
In the darkness
Of their abandonment.
Unlucky at love,
You sacrificed ribs to form
Stepmothers. Truth was,
You needed nursing
More than me.
They left us too.

You've been climbing mountains
But mostly falling down.
You're not alone...I'm right behind you.
I know, Daddy. I know.

AFTER THE QUAKE

"After the Quake"— is an emotional poem about Haiti, the earth-
quake, being Haitian, my relationship with my Mother... it is intense.
Years later, this poem still brings me to tears. I wanted to propose
a wine that will provide moments of relief to the reader. There is an
approach to food and wine pairing that suggests a simple unassum-
ing wine with a flavorful dish so that the two (wine and food) are not
competing. Pairing a high alcohol red wine with a spicy dish will exag-
gerate the heat. Instead, slightly sweet or fruity wine is suggested to
cool the hotness. I applied this method to this pairing and selected
the 1989 Domaine Leflaive Batard-Montrachet. There's nothing simple
or unassuming about this Grand Cru exquisiteness. However, the wine
possesses a tranquility that will steady the turmoil of the poem.

God's hands extended.
An invitation,
"Vini Petite, come."
An obedient moon lit my homecoming;
A child-sized tub steadied by beams waited
In the center of their circle. My father in the shadows.
Grandmother reached out to me.

"Sak a'p paser grann?"
The language rolled off my memory and rumbled the moist soil.
Vini Petite! She was relieved not to be forgotten.
A smile cracked the tension.

In the tub
The women scrubbed my body with citronella leaves.
The one scrubbing my back introduced herself, *"Je suis ton pere."*
The one splashing my face with water shouted, *"Mwen se piti ou."*

The one washing my hair whispered, *"I am you."*
And you and you and
You were there,
Watching me outgrow the tub,
Letting me leave,
Then praying for me to come home.

While I was in the wilderness,
You sang, "Ou ale, Kilè ou ap vini wè m 'ankò.
Ou ale. Kilè ou ap vini wè m 'ankò," and prayed.

You prayed and sent me dancing
Into your memory. I stumbled in
Your footsteps and danced with lost souls.
No angels lived there,
Just sun-dried bodies,
Soaking up my sweat.
And I and I and I was there,
Dancing on God's ashes.
Feeling for tears between toes.

After the quake

You were there.
Rubbing my bruised feet with oil,
Anointing them with your rain.
And you sang,
"Ou ale, Kilè ou ap vini wè m 'ankò.
Ou ale. Kilè ou ap vini wè m 'ankò," and prayed.

God's hands extended.
"Vini cheri. Dansez avec moin."
I turned away.
The sky shouts, *"Liberte pou Haiti!"*

A sudden silence.
Earth fills with the sharp scent of decay.
Jesus wept,
"Peyi a, peyi a, peyi a fin tonbe."
(He cried.)
And sent me dancing into your memories.

There were no gold-paved streets,
Just your living ashes
Holding footsteps in place.
And I was there,
Dancing on the ashes of kings,
Singing of revolution,
Chasing echoes between songs.

After the quake

You were there,
Rubbing my feet with oil,
Anointing them with your rain.
And you prayed,
"Ou ale, Kilè ou ap vini wè m 'ankò.
Ou ale. Kilè ou ap vini wè m 'ankò," and prayed.

God's hands extended.
He begs me, "Vini. Vini."
I scream, *"Lavalas!"*
Grandmother rests.
The souls of my people weep,
"Peyi a, Peyi a, Peyi a fin tonbe.
Peyi a, Peyi a, Peyi a congole."
Father joins,
"Mais a gaye roi est roi.

Mais a gaye ti mon tout mon prend loi."
My people wept
And sent me dancing
To your womb.
I followed their moans to you.
"Peyi a, Peyi a, Peyi a fin tonbe."
They sang their last rites.
"Peyi a, Peyi a, Peyi a fin tonbe."
There were so many children.
Old souls,
Regathering God's ashes.

After the quake

You…
You…
You are here,
Your hands extended,
Anointing, healing, and
Praying me back to God, singing,
" Ou ale, Kilè ou ap vini wè m 'ankò.
Ou ale. Kilè ou ap vini wè m 'ankò."

CLAUDIA

"Claudia" is written for my cousin, who was trapped in a house fire and survived, but she has never been the same since. Her poem needed wine that matches the impact of her life then and now. Of course, the Cantina Oliena 'Corrasi.' An enormous, defiant, mouth-coating wine with flavors of dark berries, spices, vanilla, and smoke that graciously glides across the tongue.

Sister, you were in my head all morning. No time for your eccentricity—I quieted my intuition with a glass of mimosa and a late-afternoon nap.

Sunlight, an urgent wake-up call, crept through the blinds, forcing my eyes open on your behalf. Later. Later. Later. A pillow over my face restored my peace of mind.

Desperate, you used your last breath to summon our grandmother's spirit to me. Her cry, the chattering of sixteen birds outside my window, I can never ignore.

"Regine," she called out to me. "Leve...wake up," she translated, in case I'd forgotten how to speak Creole. "Leve..." She shook me from the darkness.
I knew right away.
Faith turned her back on God.

You dreamed you were asleep, the smoke and fire invitations from both heaven and hell. You've always been somewhere in the middle. Half saint, half sinner. Your war was fought on temple grounds and corners of temptation.

I sat through your breaking. Watched you run through altar calls, searching for salvation and a high. Begging for a laying on of hands but settling for a quick lay. The devil is a liar.

I listened to you un-hem over dinner, in the bed next to mine, and over the phone. I saw you falling and ran home shaken—another AWOL soldier. I didn't know what to do.

Were you sitting in bed, and the last thread came loose with no "Lord there to hem you in behind and before…no hand to lay upon you"?

Was your darkness so heavy that even God could not find you?
      And our laughter burned to ashes.
I phoned too late. I called just in time.
"Claudia. Claudia, it's me. Wake up. Leve."
"Oh my God…" you screamed, and the phone went dead.

They tell me I saved you, and I have recreated that day a thousand times, speculating on what happened and how. Speaking with an audacity reserved for the dead.

But you're still alive. Still fighting the middle, still frozen in purgatory, flirting with angels and demons.

They said you were smoking in bed. You were drowsy from an overdose and let a cigarette burn. "We tried to get her to quit," they absolve themselves. "She had too much demon in her. Always has, since she was a baby."

"You were cursed," they said, "cast out of heaven," and they offered your life as evidence. There was an intruder, a lover that set your sheets on fire. Maybe it was the lover's girlfriend.

Their theories are fairy tales. I spent that last week with you.

I stay quiet, afraid to question their understanding of God. Afraid to question his will, lest He leave me in the darkness.

I dream of you surrounded in sunlight, balanced on the edge of a mountain. You tip forward and backward with the wind. Our stories and laughter circled around you. No grandmother, no phones...You're too far...gone.

I'm sorry. I'm sorry. I'm sorry. Claudia.
Oh my God...I have no words...
What if the phoenix never rises?

MATANTE CLAUDE

Written for my generous aunt—she always seems to find the money, time, and love to give to everyone in need. I celebrate her with the Monchhof Estate Riesling. The wine is light and restful, with refreshing lime, honey, and stone fruits. Like my Aunt Claude, this wine consoles and makes you forget all that is wrong in the world.

Lost spirits shelter
in the small of her back.
They camp
along its river,
Plant trees,
and make homes.
"Pack light," she prays
and makes room for their children.

MY CHILDREN

This poem is a love letter and an apology to the children I didn't have. There is both regret and longing in this piece. The Piedmont Guy Vino Blanco, an unfiltered Arneis. both raw and lovely mirrored the poem. As with "My Children," there is a duality to this wine; the sour-apple notes complement the yearning in the piece, while the lovely floral flavors match my imagination.

I would have named you Sarai,
Called you Angel, and slipped
Sugar cubes of confidence into
Your cereal. I would have loved
You more than…even when…and
Yes, afterward. We would have
Shared dreams, secrets, and okay,
Okay, my favorite dress. I would
Have, I could have, should have.
I wish, I wish, I wish.

EMANUEL AND ANASTASIA

Light, easy, pure, and sweet like children's laughter, "Emmanuel and Anastasia" is paired with Saracco Moscato d'Asti.

> Angels
> tiptoe onto earth,
> on the high notes
> of Saturday night's laughter,
> and sprinkle
> fairy dust on our
> dilapidated Sundays.

For Lupita

JARVIS

The reference to Africa in this poem made Pinotage, South Africa's signature grape, an obvious choice. The Robertson Family Oval Ranch, Pinotage for its smooth tempo. This wine starts off with plums and dark fruit on the palate and then reveals flavors of bananas and strawberries. Just when you think it's done, it closes with an earthy, smoky finish.

Suspicious of words, you choose to
Connect rhythms to God and ask for "mercy."
You found Africa in your hair and
Played for her deliverance. Hallelujah.

Man-child, your drum beats
Hope, calling the Holy Spirit to dance
Like shadows. We offered our prayers
Through tears and heard
God tapping his feet in approval. "Well done, my boy.
Well done." Amen.

SARAI

This poem is about the struggle between the adult self and the child within. I paired it with larger-than-life Laurent-Perrier Rose Champagne. Damn it's delicious. This champagne has an opulent, dazzling pink hue. The palate is sophisticated and rich with cherry, strawberry, red berry flavors integrated with chalky soil. Simply gorgeous, indulgent and provides a pure bliss.

My childhood sits on cloud nine beside me in an electric-pink dress, the heels of her white shoes clicking against our bedpost. This is her music. My childhood swings her head in a timeless rhythm, encouraged by the heaviness of her long braids bouncing off her shoulders. I fear her vanity will destroy her: she never says thank you after a compliment. So I tell her adult stories of fading beauty and loss of power. The "*enfant*" licks and swings through my stories, so I show her my grown-up scars and pictures of their development. She clicks and swings at my scars, so I tender letters as evidence. She clicks and swings through my letters, and we go on with this scuffle.

She must be counseled.

RONALD

Cantele Primitivo pairs with the poem "Ronald." I chose Primitivo because it is the father of the Zinfandel grape. Both Zinfandel and Primitivo derive from the Croatian grape Crljenak. In my opinion, Primitivo doesn't have as much depth and power as Zinfandel. Instead, it has an earthiness; it is more settled. I imagine like a father, like my brother Ronald, the Primitivo gave up some of its power for the sake of his children.

My brother
Fathers babies!
My brother, a father—
Oh brother!
Our father
Never brothered us
As babies.
So you, brother,
Father me.

YO' MAMA

This poem is so shocking that I needed a wine that is as expressive. I selected the Astrolabe Sauvignon Blanc. The fruit echoes the sweet innocence of our child narrator and the focused acidity the bitterness of his circumstances.

He tells a story of his Mama and a Coca-Cola bottle.
His Mama is bad and strong.
My father was trying to bully Mama, right.
He pulled her dress up over her face
And twisted it on top of her head.
He started laughing.
"Stop! Not in my house, Nig**r!"
Mama ripped that dress off her head and grew six feet.

A Coca-Cola bottle for a sword, half-empty, to Father's temple.
She drops the bottle.
"No, Mama, pick it back up!"

He does not tell this part of the story.
Father gets away with a scar,
But she is spinning, spinning, spinning,
Drinking from bottles.

He hates the smell of Coca-Cola on her breath.
I don't like the way it tastes," he says.
She takes a sip.
The boy is angry and remembers the story his way.
A Coca-Cola bottle, half-full, to Father's temple.

Mama took that bottle and swung it at him.
He never bullied her again. Right.
"What happened to the Coke bottle?" I ask.
He rolls his eyes at my cynicism and remembers
The story his way.

He needs her like that.
He sees himself as his father and screams from the pain.
He sees himself as his mother and grows weak from dizziness.

"I'll find it for you, Mama," he promises.
"I'll find it."
She takes a sip.

He brought a bottle to her.
Her fingers could not grasp it.
"This ain't the right one."
She spins. He apologizes.
"I'll find it, Mama. I'll find it."
She takes a sip.

He brought her another bottle.
She did not recognize.
"This ain't my drink."
She spins. He agrees.
"That's not how I remember it either.
I'll find it, Mama. I'll find it."
She takes a sip.

Still he is searching, searching, searching for her bottle,
As they, mother and son, grow weak from dizziness.
She from sipping. He from searching.
They are spinning, spinning, spinning,
And Father walked away with a scar.

PART 3
BLUE NUDES

WATCHING HER

I needed a loud, catcalling kind of wine to pair with the desire in this poem. Cuvelier Los Andes Malbec is muscular: a sinewy, peppery, dark berry blast that spanks you with a hot leather strap.

His
Silence curves beneath the peak
Of her breast—rattles daisies
Loose from her hair,
Swirls around her hips,
"Taps that ass,"
And
Ruptures along the surface of her leg.
She is still.
He collapses, bent on bare back.
A fault line is drawn.

JEAN LOVES NICOLE

"Jean Loves Nicole" with Theopolis Vineyards Petite Sirah. This wine like this poem is full of attitude—a disarming, full-bodied, big-hipped, chewy wine that shouts, "Pay attention to me!"

He's
snappin'
and
whistlin'
To join in the funk
Of the swing-swing rhythm
In your dancing hips.
Go on girl, shake that thang.
He is swaying to join in your swing.

FOLIA

At lunch with a former lover, I noticed, for the first time, this deep break at the base of his neck. It fascinated me; at that moment, all I could imagine was pressing my tongue into this space. Paired with the W & J Graham's 10-Year-Old Tawny Port. Like this port, he is the color of amber. His skin tasted like caramel, chocolate, and sea salt when we made love.

> Fuck this fu-fu Italian ice cream.
> I'd rather lick clean the bowl at the base of your neck.
> Yesterday at lunch,
> Thrill number 742—the absence
> At the meeting of your collarbones.
> In between conversations and bites of
> Mocha-truffle-pecan-caramel-praline gelato,
> My tongue tied, crazy to taste your hollowness.
> Amazing—
> The butterflies have not abandoned me.
> Two years, twelve days, and
> A few hours to spare.
> I'm still counting the ways
> You thrill me.

REVEREND FEELGOOD

"Reverend Feelgood" is heightened by the Alexander Valley Sin Zin. Well, yes, the name made it an obvious choice for this poem. Also, this wine is sexy, with cherry-red flavors, like the taste of our main character's kiss. This wine is spicy, with plum, black pepper, and chocolate powder.

You had your stuff together—getting on that pulpit each day, calling us sinners, looking down on our wicked ways. You've been preaching 'bout fornication, obeying God's laws, being strong enough to fight temptation. We were all impressed by your youthful devotion until that summer's day when God sent you a test—Deseray Belle in a tight red dress.

That day you was working over in the projects. You heard Deseray Belle's soft sweet singing coming from her Mama's third-floor apartment. You turned around to see her plump black cherry-red lips wanting, aching to drink the sweat from your chest. All you wanted to do was escape the devil heat and melt into hers. But that gold cross carrying that pure, innocent, virtuous Jesus you've been preaching 'bout burned at your heart. You felt God's ice-cold blue eyes watching you wanting Deseray.

You got on your knees and asked God to save you from temptation, but God would not be petitioned. He was tired of you being his competition. God stood on that mountain, laughing at your tears. He'd been waiting, waiting to get you all these years.

Never seen a grown man cry so hard before, praying for a little loving on the floor, crying to be baptized again in Deseray's sweet sweat of sin. I must confess you did your best. But young, plump, sweet-smelling Deseray got to smiling and switching, dancing and prancing. Made you feel a tremor in your pants; you forgot God and preaching and learned to dance.

Tried to keep it quiet so we and the Lord wouldn't hear your moaning and groaning—even had some nerve to keep judging. "Fight temptation, Saints—fight," you preached.

Kept it quiet till Sister Belle rocked you right, and we all heard you preaching "Oh my…oh my…oh my *God*" all night.

RON CHILDS

I love this piece because it truly captures the character of Ron Childs.
But which wine? I traveled the globe, mentally searching for the appro-
priate pairing. Then by chance, I tasted the Vision Cellars Red Blend.
An opulent blend of Cabernet Sauvignon, Petit Verdot, Merlot, Malbec
and Cabernet Franc. With every sip, the wine offers another layer of
flavors—dark berries, cola, chocolate, and sweet oak. With every sip,
it opens up another path to explore.

> He searches the cracks
> Of her language for
> Secret passageways
> And underground railroads.
> Her pauses,
> Doubtful silences, part seas
> And pave roads to heaven.
>
> Some of us remember home.

TANYA

Tanya's favorite body part is her thick, long, and heavy curls. It is the first thing that most notice when they meet her. I wanted a wine that would contrast the heaviness of hair. I relied upon the Domaine de l'Ecu Muscadet, a dry, light-bodied, acidic wine having green citrus and green-apple fruit flavors and a touch of saline.

Longing weaves a river
Through her hair.
She tosses
The heavy strands
From a castle in the sky
To his lips.
Come to…
He has never
Tasted holy water.

ROBERT COURTS PAM

I'll never forget the happiness in Robert's voice when he told me about the night he met Pam. His story was so full of excitement, humor, and confidence that I had to capture it in a poem. The Veuve Clicquot, Demi-Sec Champagne, a sweet, racy wine, that effortlessly matches the energy of this modern-day courtship.

As certain as a dozen
Red roses, without the loss of
$54.95 or Shakespearean cliché,
Robert's witty tongue wiggles
Tickling truths about Pam's
Beauty, booty, and the color of brownies.

Her other suitors fell short. Beaming bling and bartering baubles for back. A Renaissance woman, Pam was working a plan, searching for a beacon and beads.

With each giggle, she goes gaga, growing powerless to Robert's praises—*having heard them before*, but never with this much je ne sais quoi.

Pen and paper in hand, the other men watch, amazed by Robert's power of persuasion. "What did he say?" they scrambled. "Man, did you get that?"

Rob's victory cry—"I do. I do. I do, you sexy motherfucker."

PROVERBS FOR DANITA

Pinot Noir grape is difficult to cultivate. It is thin skinned which makes it susceptible to vineyard hazards. It requires a regimen of cool morning, warm afternoons and cool foggy nights. Like a bruised heart, with gentle and precise care these fragile grapes can be loved into producing life altering libations. I offer The Joseph Drouhin Côte de Nuits-Village, a gorgeous wine with notes of berries, baked spices, mushrooms, and cherry to my friend Danita.

Red-wine halo erases a stormy beginning.
He who is the one sees past your winter, rips at solitude's dress, braids his body to yours, your bodies to vines, while autumn leaves chant sacred melodies above your heads.

Surrender to love's embrace, and earth will breathe a white chiffon morning.

NANCY

Only a passionate wine could match Nancy's unsettling spirit, something that moves like fire and feels insatiable. The Chateau de Beaucastel, Côtes du Rhône Coudoulet Rouge, is her match. Lush with dark berries, licorice, pepper, and lavender, this wine, like Nancy, is limitless.

She watches fires
Travel the roads of her palm.
Sirens sound suitors to slide
down poles to her rescue.
The first had a hose. The second
a blanket. The third a ring.
We are amused. This fire won't
cool.

FINDING NATALYN

Even a meat and potatoes, dry red wine lover will fall for Chateau d'Yquem Sauternes. This bright gold liquid is rich with flavors of spiced honey and vanilla. One of the most extraordinary wines you'll ever taste.

Chocolate isn't always bitter.

He found butterscotch in between her lips, a lingering of ginger on her skin, a touch of vanilla in her talk, and sugar on her walls.

Must be jelly, cause jam don't shake like that. Jelly roll…jelly roll. Never knew he had a sweet tooth.

Sugar Mama, Sugar Mama, where you been?

LOVE

The mood of the poem "Love" is playful and carefree. Love asks us to "forget the hour" or forget our past and lose ourselves for a moment. I choose Vinho Verde white wine because they are best when experienced young. They don't require that we delay our gratification but allow us to indulge now. The Quinta da la Lixa, Vinho Verde, a happy-go-lucky wine with a light spritz, a lovely floral nose, bright acidity, and a touch of sea salt that gives it a certain unexpected cleverness.

Forget the hour—
Let's rain blue waves,
Whisper waters into rivers,
Share oceans—taste mangos in the sea
While our reason drifts toward the shore.

Let's make angels in an abstract painting,
Free-fall tandem under a new spell—
Tango in an open stream.
Surf the wind's music
For one night.

End this wilderness—
I want to wing over stars.
Exhale a sunny day—fly orchards.
Trail silence
While a crescent moon bursts into laughter
And I slip a few poems into your front pocket.

The End

WINE LIST

Château Musar Gaston Hochar, Bekaa Valley, Lebanon
Yalumba Eden Valley Viognier, Barossa, Australia
Inman Family Endless Crush® OGV Estate Rosé of Pinot Noir, Santa Rosa, CA
Kendall Jackson Vintner's Reserve Chardonnay, USA
Allegrini Amarone della Valpolicella Classico D.O.C., Veneto, Italy
Domaine Zind-Humbrech Gewurztraminer Turckheim, Alsace, France
Conundrum White, California, U.S.A
Marchesi Antinori Villa Antinori Chianti Classico Riserva, Tuscany, Italy
E. Guigal Condrieu, Rhone, France
Coto de Gomariz "The Flower and The Bee" Treixadura,
Brown Estate Vineyards Chaos Theory, Napa Valley, California, U.S.A
Emilio Lustau 'Solera Reserva' Los Arcos Dry Amontillado Sherry, Andalusia, Spain
Silice, D.O. Riberia Sacra, Spain
Movia Lunar 8 Ribolla, Slovenia
Casa Ferreirinha "Papa Figos" Tinto, Douro, Portugal
Maison Noir O.P.P., Other People's Pinot "Noir", Willamette Valley, Oregon, U.S.A
Don Rodolfo Art of the Andes, Tannat, Mendoza, Argentina
1989 Domaine Leflaive Batard-Montrachet, Grand Cru, Cote de Baune, France
Cantina Oliena 'Corrasi' Nepente di Oliena Cannonau di Sardegna Riserva, Sardina, Italy
Monchhof Estate Riesling, Mosel, Germany
The Piedmont Guy Vino Blanco, Piedmont, Italy
Saracco Moscato d'Asti DOCG, Piedmont, Italy
Robertson Family Oval Ranch, Pinotage, South Africa
Champagne Laurent-Perrier Cuvee Rose, France

Cantele Primitivo Salento IGT Puglia, Italy
Astrolabe Province Malborough Sauvignon Blanc, New Zealand
Cuvelier Los Andes Grand Malbec, Vista Flores, Argentina
Theopolis Vineyards Petite Sirah, Yorkville, Highlands, California, USA
W & J Graham's 10 Year-Old Tawny Port, Portugal
Alexander Valley Vineyards Sin Zin Zinfandel I, Alexander Valley, California, USA
Can Blau Monstant, Spain
Domaine de l'Ecu Muscadet Serve-et-Maine Cuvee Classique, Loire Valley, France
Veueve Clicquot Demi-Sec Champagne, France
Joseph Drouhin Côte de Nuits-Village, Burgundy, France
Chateau de Beaucastel Côtes du Rhône Coudoulet Rouge, AOC, Rhône Valley, France
Chateau d'Yquem Sauternes, France
Quinta da la Lixa, 'Aroma de Castas', Vinho Verde, Portugal

ABOUT THE AUTHOR

Regine T. Rousseau is a proud Haitian American poet, author, somme-lier, and businesswoman. She is the CEO of Shall We Wine, an event-planning and wine-demonstration company based in Chicago, Illinois.

Rousseau received her bachelor's degree from Knox College. She re-ceived her Level II certification from the International Sommelier Guild and an Executive Bourbon Steward from Stave and Thief Society.

Rousseau enjoys traveling, cooking, spending time with her beloved niece and nephew, and educating others in the art of wine tast-ing. For more information about her work, she invites you to visit RegineRousseau.com and ShallWeWine.com.

11063913R00046

Made in the USA
Monee, IL
06 September 2019